When referencing financial, marketing or sales information in any of our books, websites, blogs, videos, resources, newsletters, and any other content, we have taken every effort to ensure we've accurately represented ideas, theories, products and services, and their ability to improve the success of your business and your life.

We offer no guarantee that you will get the results you seek to use these ideas, tools and strategies. We do not engage in 'get rich quick' schemes or ideas. We also do not guarantee earnings.

It is up you, as the reader, how much time and energy are spent applying the following information. It is also your choice whether you take on board and follow through with any business or marketing idea/advice, and you should recognise that a number of factors will affect any success achieved.

You, as the reader, are responsible for your own actions and outcomes. We are merely representing generic ideas from industry experts that we believe, when acted upon, create differing degrees of success.

Finally, we recommend that you seek advice from the appropriately qualified professionals, i.e. solicitors, accountants, doctors or psychologists if specific help is required, pertinent to your individual circumstances.

About the Author

Heather Robinson has been helping businesses and organisations get the most out the internet since 2005. Helping them to define and implement effective marketing strategies, manage budgets, and deliver the best results possible in line with achieving their goals.

As a marketing graduate, Heather has worked in all areas of marketing, but her passion lies with digital technologies. She effectively utilises platforms such as Google AdWords, social media networks and email marketing to maximise exposure for her clients and drive a constant flow of traffic to their websites.

In 2012, Heather set up 'Skittish', a boutique digital agency, in order to help small to medium sized businesses gain a good grasp of all the opportunities available to them in the online world. Her clients vary from 'one-man-band' and micro businesses to larger, multinational companies.

A lot of Heather's time is dedicated to delivering training and talks in her area of expertise, running regular workshops aimed at business owners in areas such as email marketing strategy and creating a content marketing plan. She also regularly speaks at local, national and global digital marketing conferences and has contributed to Essential Digital Marketing for Small Business, by Simon Dunant (2014).

Email Marketing Success:
Build Trust. Win Customers.

by
Heather Robinson

First published in 2015 by:

The Solopreneur Publishing Company Ltd.
West Yorkshire WF9 1PB
www.thesolopreneur.co.uk

ISBN 978-0-9931880-6-0

Printed in the U.K. by Charlesworth Press, Flanshaw Lane,
Wakefield WF2 9LP

PUBLISHER'S DISCLAIMER

CONTACT HEATHER:

Facebook: /SkittishConsultancy
Twitter: @_skittish
Email: heather@skitti.sh
Web-site: http://skitti.sh

ABOUT THE 'SOLOPRENEUR'S GUIDE' SERIES

This book - indeed, every book in the 'Solopreneur's Guide' series - is different from most other business guides or titles. It's not structured chapter by chapter; instead, the content is laid out in such a way that it answers solopreneurs' most frequently asked questions on a given topic or discipline.

So, what is a 'solopreneur'?

The term 'solopreneur' is used when talking about 'Independent Professionals' (or 'IPs'). There are many similarities between solopreneurs and entrepreneurs; in the context of our books and series, by describing a business owner as a solopreneur, we're referring to people who are completely reliant on their own personal brand in order to make a living (essentially, 'one-person-brands').

What else is unique about the 'Solopreneur's Guide' series?

When researching the merit of business books, feedback showed that solopreneurs found many titles hard to relate to – particularly those written by successful, or well-known, business leaders. Though solopreneurs felt some information within these books was valuable, they said the 'golden nuggets' were hidden by masses of pretentious, technical, or irrelevant text. They were also disappointed that the majority of business books failed to offer direction on how to apply the authors' advice within the average solopreneur business. As a result, the business owners we spoke to felt that many authors of non-fiction 'business books' didn't understand them or their needs.

Most businesses – even global corporations – have to start somewhere. Having a small business does not mean the owner has little ambition, nor is it a measure of how successful the business will remain as time advances. The right kind of information, applied at the right time, will help more businesses grow – which is where this series comes in. We've sourced the best experts in each field: qualified and experienced professionals - whose target markets are made up of solopreneurs and small business owners – who will impart useful, appropriate information, in an easy-to-apply format.

In today's society, people want to fast-track their understanding of a subject and any subsequent results. The advent of the Internet has made knowledge more accessible than ever, but nothing can replace the added ingredient of experience within that framework.

The authors chosen to write for the 'Solopreneur's Guide' series are already recognised experts with a credible track record. They understand their customers – and, in turn, their readers - and the problems they commonly face.

These experts are accessible, which we feel is important, should you like more information or tailored advice. They're not unattainable or out of reach – all 'Solopreneur's Guide' authors are business owners, just like you. Contact information will be included in all books, relating to the author in question, as well as links to any free downloads/resources/training in the ABOUT THE AUTHOR section, at the beginning of each book.

Every 'Solopreneur's Guide' author is active on social media and welcomes your feedback.

CONTENTS

Other titles in the series.

Introduction

Email marketing has become somewhat overshadowed in recent years by the rise of social media, with many new and existing businesses choosing to focus their efforts on establishing themselves on platforms such as Facebook, Twitter and YouTube, rather than incorporate email communications into their marketing mix.

This, I believe, comes down to what is 'trendy' at the time. Social media certainly has its place in an effective marketing strategy, but it seems wrong to overlook the other forms of digital marketing that have served us so well over the years. It may also be down to email marketing losing favour with marketers and business owners given the sheer number of emails we all receive on a daily basis.

Emails are often perceived as SPAM, simply because we have too many in our inbox or we don't remember signing up for a list. Some would say that any email from a company trying to sell something is SPAM, but that is simply not the case. There are many emails I receive from companies that I look forward to receiving and reading. And, yes, I have purchased products and services off the back of an email campaign. I'm sure this is the case for most recipients, so you shouldn't be perturbed about sending emails to your database. You just need to make sure it's your email they look forward to receiving and reading!

While I encourage everyone to use email as part of their marketing strategy, there are a few things you need to be aware of before you start. There are also lots of things you need to keep in mind while you implement a plan. In this book, I'll be covering the benefits of using email communications over other forms of marketing (including social media!). Also, I will include what you need to know about the law surrounding email communications, both in the EU and the US.

I'll then look at starting a list of email subscribers or adding to an existing list, and the different methods you can use to make sure the people on your list are the people who want to receive your emails.

Once you have your list, you need to consider which email marketing software to use to send your emails. In chapter 4 I'll explain why it's essential to invest in bespoke software rather than relying on Outlook, Gmail, or Hotmail, to send bulk emails.

Chapter 5 will give you some pointers on how to get your email into the inbox (rather than the junk folder). I will give you tips on what to avoid to make sure your email isn't labelled as SPAM and filtered or deleted. I'll then look at how you can get your email opened. It's great to get your email into the inbox, but if it never gets opened, you have lost an opportunity to get in front of someone who could just be your next customer.

And finally, I'll look at the reports you will get from your email marketing software that will give you an indication as to how well your campaign has performed. I'll explain what the terms mean and also how to improve your next campaign if the last one didn't perform as you had hoped.

By the end of this book, you should feel confident in setting up your first email campaign to your database and know how to optimise your email content to get the best results possible. If you have been using email marketing for a while, you should be more confident at creating campaigns that will continue to bring you results.

Chapter One:
Why and when should I use email over other forms of marketing?

Email marketing can fit into just about any marketing plan, but it's essential that it's used at the right point in the sales cycle and that you are clear on your goals. In this chapter, I'll look at where and how to incorporate email marketing into your strategy and how it fits with other forms of marketing. But, first of all, let's look at why you should be using email marketing in the first place.

According to McKinsey & Company,

"Email remains a significantly more effective way of acquiring new customers than social media - nearly 40 times that of Facebook and Twitter combined."
(Source: McKinsey & Co, 2014 http://bit.ly/mckinseyandco)

40 times! I'm sure you'll agree, that's a huge advantage that email has over social media.

What's important to note here is that what McKinsey & Co. are measuring is the ability to "acquire customers". Social media is itself a fantastic tool that should be a part of your marketing activities too, but it's a tool for another job when it comes to acquiring customers.

Social media plays a huge role in reaching new

people, engaging with potential customers, building a following and developing brand advocates. However, generating direct sales from social media is a little more difficult. It's not impossible by any means, but the nature of social media is that it's 'social' and people expect businesses to be social too.

No one likes to be sold to, especially when they are not in the market for buying something. As people trawl through their Facebook newsfeed, they are not looking to purchase something at that moment in time, so by advertising in a very 'salesy' way you can turn people off.

Using Facebook advertising in other ways, for instance, to build your followers or increase engagement on your posts, can be a lot more effective.

By using social media in this way, you can build up a relationship with your followers before you begin your email campaigns.

So, let's look at the sales process and how different forms of marketing fit into each stage. Here I will use the 'AIDA' model. AIDA stands for Awareness, Interest, Desire and Action and describes how people go through each phase in turn in the buying process (see http:// en.wikipedia.org/wiki/AIDA_%28marketing%29).

Awareness

Before someone can purchase something from you, whether it's a product or service, they must become aware of you, your business and have a vague idea of what you do. So how do you get people to become aware of you?

Social media is fantastic for this phase as you can get your message out in front of lots of people. You could use email marketing here if you've purchased a list of email addresses, even though they will not yet know who you are.

Some companies will use print advertising, TV advertising or trade shows as a way to increase their brand awareness. However, these methods can be costly.

Interest

Now you want to tell people about what you do and match your products and services with their needs. If you are successful in doing that, you will then find that your potential customers will start to show an interest in what you do and how you can help them solve their problems.

This is where social media needs to be taken to the next level and need to take people away from Facebook and Twitter and onto your email mailing list. Ideally, you'll be driving traffic back to your website from your social media channels through links, articles and promotions. This traffic should then be encouraged to sign up for your email newsletter. If they are interested in your products and services at this point, then they are likely to want to receive updates and deals directly into their inbox. Make sure you ask for their email details to enable you to do this.

Desire

Here is where your potential customers are not only interested in what you can offer, but they also have a desire to buy from you. Email marketing fits extremely well into this stage, as it's a great way to send targeted sales messages to your email database. You can segment your lists to target people based on their characteristics and send emails containing messages aimed directly at individuals that have shown an interest in your products and services.

Action

It's at this stage where your potential customers become actual customers, and they go ahead and purchase something from you or enquire about your services. This likely to be through your website or over the phone, but your email campaigns have been an important instrument for taking your customers through each stage of the AIDA model.

Social Media Today state that "Consumers who receive marketing emails spend 83% more [than those that don't." (source: http://bit.ly/

mktgemails). 83% is potentially a huge increase in sales and enquiries for any business, so if you're not investing time in email marketing, why not?

Email Vs. Other Marketing Activities

Email provides other benefits too when compared to other forms of marketing. For example, emails can be targeted at individuals who are likely to buy your products, and your email will land in their personal inbox and remain there until it's opened.

With social media, your updates can be sent out and often feel more like a scatter-gun approach; not knowing whether the right people are seeing and reading your updates and whether they are relevant to those who do read them.

There's also the issue of the newsfeed and the speed at which it moves for most people. Sending just one tweet a day could mean that very few people are online at that particular time to read it, and by the time they do check in your tweet has gone. With email, sending just one a week is more than enough.

When compared to more traditional forms of marketing such as direct mail, email marketing poses a number of benefits; the first being design costs. If you were to produce a flyer or brochure to send out to your database, you'd need to invest in a graphic designer to produce the artwork.

With email, you can use a pre-set template that will save you time and costs.

A direct mail campaign would also incur print costs on top of postage costs that could go into the thousands depending on the size of your database. With email marketing, you can send out emails for free with MailChimp, providing your list is less than 2,000 people. Even with a larger list, expect to pay around 1p per email. Compare that to the price of a postage stamp, and you can easily see how cost effective email marketing can be.

The other problem with direct mail is tracking the results. It becomes very difficult to see whether your mailer has been read and how many enquiries or sales happened as a direct result of the mailer being sent. With email marketing, you'll be able to track who has opened your email and clicked through to your website, providing you with valuable information to improve your marketing campaigns.

If I look at another form of traditional marketing, telesales, then email provides a much more time effective way of contacting a large number of people at the same time. It can also be less intrusive and avoids interrupting people at a time that isn't convenient to them. An email will reach the person and sit in their inbox until they are ready to open it. No one wants to receive a sales call when they're in the middle of something really important, but receiving an email has less of an impact on the busy person receiving it, as it can be ignored until a more convenient time.

Email marketing is something that can have the biggest impact in terms of sales, with the least amount of time required. Social media requires you to invest time each day in sending out updates, replying to people and engaging in the conversation. A direct mail campaign could take days and weeks to plan, design, print and mail. Telesales would require for you to be on the phone for hours at a time to reach as many people as you could in just seconds with an email campaign.

An email can be set up and sent out in under an hour and only needs to be done once a week or once a month, depending on your schedule and what fits with you and your audience. You should then schedule in some time to review the campaign and see how many people opened and responded to the email, but this should take no longer than half an hour.

So not only is email marketing a cheaper alternative to other forms of traditional marketing, it's also less time intensive and performs better at acquiring new customers.

Other benefits include being able to easily personalise emails so they look less like a bulk email campaign. You can add in 'merge fields' (these will be familiar to those who have ever done a mail merge in Microsoft Word). These fields correspond to the data you have in your database. So if you have a field for 'First Name', 'Last Name', 'Email Address', 'Company Name', 'Date of last order', etc., you can include this information in each email you send out, simply by placing a merge field in the email where you want the data to appear, and the email software will do the rest for you.

For example, your email could be personalised like this, where the merge fields appear between curly brackets:

Hi {first_name}

Thank you for your order on {order_date}. We hope you were pleased with your purchase and would like to offer you a discount off your next order.

So if {company_name} requires any additional supplies from us, please quote DISC10 to receive 10% off your next order.

Have a great day!

Once your email is sent, the recipient will receive something like this:

Hi Heather

Thank you for your order on 15 January. We hope you were pleased with your purchase and would like to offer you a discount off your next order.

*So if Skittish requires any additional supplies
from us, please quote DISC10 to receive 10% off
your next order.*

Have a great day!

Email marketing is also a great way to cross-sell
other complementary products or services you
provide. I met with a potential client who had
been in business for over ten years and had been
dealing with many of the same customers over
that time. He provided fire safety training, risk
assessments and also sold fire extinguishers to
commercial customers.

On an annual visit to one of the clients to carry
out their risk assessment, he noticed that they
had replaced all of their fire extinguishers for the
entire building since his last visit. He asked if
they'd mind saying who they bought them from
and why they didn't come to him for a quote.
Their reply was "we didn't know you sold them".

This customer had been with him for 10 years,
yet they were unaware of all the products and
services he provided. A simple email once in a
while to his existing database could have meant
that he had a chance to win that business and
continue to build the relationship with that client.

How many of your existing customers know
all of the services you offer? Perhaps you're

a web designer who also offers search engine optimisation, or a photographer who also does video production, or a PR consultant who also produces blog content for clients, or even a life coach that also offers hypnotherapy.

Sending someone a quick email that outlines what you offer, could mean the difference between getting a new client, or losing one to a competitor.

Email provides the perfect medium to keep in touch with existing customers, build the relationship and generate repeat business. It's also great for nurturing relationships with potential customers and new contacts, building trust and generating an interest in your services.

After reading this chapter, I hope you feel excited and enthusiastic about email marketing, and you're now seeing it in a new light with the opportunities it brings. Before you go racing off to send your next email, there are a few legalities I need to cover in the next chapter, so keep reading!

Chapter Two:
Who can I email without breaking any anti-SPAM laws?

It's a big issue with email communications and one which we all hate - SPAM! No one wants to receive SPAM, nor do we want people to misread our email as being SPAM. This chapter will take you through how to remain compliant when sending emails and how to make sure you're never labelled as a 'spammer'.

**Disclaimer: I am not a lawyer or qualified to advise on legal matters. I, therefore, recommend that you research the laws in your country and seek professional legal advice.

In both the EU and the US, there are strict laws that govern the sending of marketing emails. In the EU (which includes the UK), we are governed by the Privacy & Electronic Communications (EC Directive) Regulations 2003. The US is governed by the CAN-SPAM Act 2003.

EU Law

Below is an excerpt from the regulations that affects businesses sending email messages to individuals for marketing purposes (emphasis added).

Use of electronic mail for direct marketing purposes
22.—(1) This regulation applies to the

transmission of unsolicited communications
by means of electronic mail to individual
subscribers.

(2) Except in the circumstances referred
to in paragraph (3), a person shall neither
transmit, nor instigate the transmission of,
unsolicited communications for the purposes
of direct marketing by means of electronic mail
unless the recipient of the electronic mail has
previously notified the sender that he consents
for the time being to such communications
being sent by, or at the instigation of, the
sender.

This states that you cannot send emails of a
marketing nature to an individual without their
explicit consent. We call this *'opting-in'*.

In some situations, this can be what's known as
a *'soft opt-in'*. To qualify as a soft opt-in, the
following criteria must be met:

(3) A person may send or instigate the sending
of electronic mail for the purposes of direct
marketing where—
(a) that person has obtained the contact details
of the recipient of that electronic mail in the
course of the sale or negotiations for the sale of
a product or service to that recipient;
(b) the direct marketing is in respect of that
person's similar products and services only;
and
(c) the recipient has been given a simple means
of refusing (free of charge except for the costs

of the transmission of the refusal) the use of
his contact details for the purposes of such
direct marketing, at the time that the details
were initially collected, and, where he did not
initially refuse the use of the details, at the
time of each subsequent communication.
(4) A subscriber shall not permit his line to be
used in contravention of paragraph (2).

In this case, you must first seek the consent of
the recipient by giving them the opportunity to
opt-out of receiving email communications.

This is important! So even if they are past
customers or clients you have worked with
recently, you must give them an opportunity to
decline marketing messages when you collect
the email address and the option to 'opt-out' of
receiving emails in the future.

It's important to note here that these regulations
apply when sending emails to individuals rather
than businesses. Sending emails to businesses
is slightly more relaxed in that you do not need
explicit consent prior to sending your first email.
Instead, you are permitted to send marketing
emails provided you give the recipient the
opportunity to opt-out on every email you send.

So, just to clarify, for business to consumer
emails (B2C), an explicit opt-in is required. For
business to business emails (B2B), opt-out is
permitted. These laws are often updated, so my
advice is always to check before sending and if

in doubt, only send to people who have opted in whether they are consumers or businesses.

US Law

If you're based in the UK or another part of Europe, you may be wondering what the US law has to do with you. Well, it's more about the email software you use, as many of the software providers are based in the US and will require that anyone who uses their software adheres to these laws too.

The CAN-SPAM Act, 2003 in the US is slightly different and works a little like the EU's B2B laws in that it's not always necessary to obtain an explicit opt-in from an individual before sending emails. Other than that, the same rule applies regarding giving every recipient the option to opt-out.

Giving people the opportunity to opt-out is simply giving them a way to 'unsubscribe' from your mailing list. This is often done by providing a link in the footer of the email that the recipient can click to be removed from the list. Or, there may be a message that asks the recipient to reply to the email with 'unsubscribe' as the subject of the email.

Either way is fine and an accepted way of letting people opt-out. When you use email marketing software such as MailChimp, this unsubscribe link is added to each and every email you send automatically, so you don't need to worry too much about including it yourself. The software takes care of it for you and ensures you never email these people again if they do choose to unsubscribe.

The CAN-SPAM Act 2003 also requires that the sender discloses their identity when sending the email and that their postal address is present on the emails they send.

When setting up your email, you are required to provide a 'From' name and email address. This should be either your name and email or your company name and an email address within your company such as info@companyname.com. It's important to be completely transparent here and not try to mislead anyone. By being open about your identity, you're not only adhering to best practice, but you could also be improving your open rates (more on that in Chapter 5!).

Having your postal address on your emails also adds credibility and provides some evidence that you are a real company with a registered office. This can add a level of reassurance to recipients so that they feel comfortable doing business with you and handing over personal information and credit card details on your website.

If you work from home, as lots of solopreneurs do, you may not want to have your home address listed on your emails and that's completely understandable both from a privacy and safety point of view.

In this instance, can I recommend that you either a). Invest in a virtual office address locally or a PO Box address. Many business centres provide virtual offices, as well as physical office space, and the cost is around £25 - £50 per month depending on the location. This often includes mail forwarding too, so you'll have the benefit of having a business address and still receiving your mail at home. Or b). Ask friends and family who have a business address that you could piggyback for a discounted rate or even for free.

When I first set up in business, I worked from the spare room (or 'Skittish HQ' as I liked to call it), and many of you may be doing so right now. It was convenient and meant I could keep costs down to a minimum. But then I had to put my address on my emails, and I just didn't feel comfortable doing that. My worst nightmare was having clients show up at the house when I'm working in my pyjamas or having people knocking on the door on evenings and weekends.

I'm sure that wouldn't have happened, but I decided to invest in a virtual office address nonetheless. The cost was an issue and as I didn't really receive much in the way of mail, I wasn't sure I wanted to pay £50 per month to have an address on an email newsletter that went out once a quarter. That would have worked out at £150 per email campaign!

Then I remembered my father who runs his own business from a local business centre just two miles from my house. So I asked him if he'd mind me using his address and him receiving the odd bit of mail for me from time to time. Well, he's my dad, so he had to say yes!

Luckily, the office space I have now is in the same building, so there's been no need to change my address. So if you're contemplating moving into your own office someday, it's worth finding where you'd like to be and see if they offer a virtual office to start with.

If you use email marketing software (and I'll discuss why you should in Chapter 4), you will be asked for your mailing address (postal not email) when you sign up and this will be used in all your emails automatically. Most software providers allow you to go back and change this so if you signed up for an account using your home address and now want to use a business address you should be able to do so in your account settings.

The key things to keep in mind when you are sending marketing emails are:
- Have the people i n your list given their consent to receiving the email (if they are individuals rather than businesses)
- Is there a way for people to unsubscribe from the list if they choose to?
- Have you disclosed your identity?
- Have you included a physical mailing address?

Once you have established that this is the case, you're then in a great position to start sending emails. If you don't have a list or your list is very small, you'll need to think about building a list that continues to grow. In the next chapter, I'll be sharing with you some ways of getting people to actively sign up to receive emails from you.

Chapter Three:
How can I build a list of subscribers?

Without a list of subscribers, your email marketing efforts would be wasted, so this chapter will give you some top tips and ideas to either start a new list of email addresses or build on an existing list.

As with most things in life, you want to focus on quality over quantity. You could have a huge database of email addresses that have been randomly collected over the years but if they are not likely to become customers in the future, they have very little value to you as a business owner.

If your list is small, but you know all the people on that list as either being past customers, present customers and people who have actively shown an interest in your products or services (e.g. requested a quotation from you or met you in the past), you'll know that your list is made up of quality email addresses.

By focusing on quality over quantity, you'll find that more people will open your emails, click and follow links in your emails and also take action and make purchases or submit enquiries.

So how do I build that list? Here I'll look at different methods of adding new people to your database. Some of these can be done 'online' (e.g. through your website) while others can be achieved 'offline' (e.g. in person).

Online methods of building your list

Website

Your website is a great place to start as you will have regular visitors to your site which are clearly interested in what you do.

To capture people's email address you can use the following techniques:

- **Newsletter sign-up form** - this adds people to a list that you can use to keep people up to date with news and special offers. If you're using a service like MailChimp, it will allow you to build the forms and embed them on your site. You may need some technical assistance with this if you don't update your website yourself, but the process is simple and shouldn't cost you an arm and a leg to have implemented.

- **Free download** - do you have a free resource such as an ebook, how-to guide, checklist or template that you could give away on your website in exchange for an email address? It could even be an informative video or audio recording that you can grant people access to once you have their information. You don't need to ask for a lot of information; just an email address (for your list) and a first name (to personalise your emails) will suffice.

- **Enquiry form** - most people, will have one of these on their website. It's a simple form for people to fill in (usually on the 'Contact Us' page) so they can send you a message through your website. This is a good, and often overlooked, way of collecting email addresses. If someone has made an enquiry through your website, they are more likely to be interested in your products or services, so it makes sense to keep in touch with these people via email.

When collecting email addresses in this way, it's a good idea to display a privacy policy on your website so people can read how you use the information you gather. They will want to know what kinds of communication to expect from you and whether their information will be used for any other purpose by any third parties (i.e. do you plan to sell their information on to other companies).

It's also good practice to get them to 'opt-in' at this point. You shouldn't assume that because someone has submitted an enquiry form on your website that they will expect to be added to a mailing list and contacted on a regular basis. Therefore, you can use wording such as:

"We'd like to keep you up to date with our latest news and offers. Please tick this box if this is ok."

Or

"By submitting your email address you are opting in to receiving further occasional emails

from us in the future."

The first option would require you to have a checkbox as part of the form where people can explicitly opt-in to your mailing list.

The second option is slightly different in that it uses the act of submitting the form to be the opt-in process.

You wouldn't need to do this if you were collecting emails as part of a newsletter subscription as it is obviously that they are signing up to receive emails from you.

Social Media

As I discussed in Chapter 1, social media plays a huge role in getting your business in front of a wider audience. They get to see what you're about and interact with you without handing over any personal information.

What you want to happen next is that they build up a level of trust with you through Facebook or Twitter and you can then direct them to a form to sign up for your newsletter, exclusive offers or some other incentive that you can provide.

Let's look at how some social media platforms can help you build your list:

• **Facebook** - with lots of email marketing software providing a Facebook sign up app, this can be a great place to start building your list. This is an application that can be added to your Facebook business page that will present your visitors with a sign-up form to fill in.

You will first need to integrate your email software with your Facebook account which can be done via your account settings. If you're having trouble finding out how to integrate with Facebook, contact your email software provider for assistance.

From your Facebook business page, browse through your **Settings** and find the **Apps** option. From here, you should now see an option to add a form to your page. This is sometimes automatic once you have integrated your accounts, in which case the App will appear down the left-hand side of your Timeline. If the app hasn't appeared automatically, click Add App to activate it on your page.

If all that sounds too complicated, how about using Facebook to drive people to your website to fill in the form there? To do this you need to create an incentive for people to click through and fill in their details, Try running competitions, offering something for free (as a downloadable resource or entry into a prize draw).

Here, the same tactics you know work on

Facebook should be used. So think about creating images and videos that will grab people's attention. Use text over your images to create easy to scan headlines that stand out from other updates. You can use free software like picmonkey.com to do this.

Also, remember to engage with your fans, ask them to share your updates and get the message out to as wide an audience as possible.

- **Twitter** - tweets can be used in the same way as Facebook updates - as a way to drive traffic to the pages on your website where you collect email addresses. Again be sure to use images as these will get better engagement, and use appropriate hashtags. (Hashtags are words or phrases preceded by the '#' symbol and they are used to categorise tweets and tell the reader what the topic of the tweet is. They also provide a way for readers to find tweets on the same topics by clicking on any hashtag).

You can also use Twitter Ads to send out tweets that collect the name and email address of people who engage with your Tweets. These are known as Lead Generation Cards and are part of the paid-for service that Twitter offers through its advertising programme.

For these campaigns to work, you need your tweets to be engaging and compelling enough that people will want what you are offering enough to hand over their email address.

- **YouTube** - creating a presence on YouTube is a fantastic way to not only get your name (and face!) out there and raise your profile, it's also a great place to build a following and direct those followers to your newsletter sign up forms and other pages on your website. You can do this by providing links on your channel and also in the descriptions of your videos.

Guest Blogging

Guest blogging is where you produce a blog post and approach blog owners and ask them to publish your post. You provide unique content for their readers and in return they will give you a section to say a little about the author and how they can find out more about you.

This is a great opportunity to add a link to your website with the sign up form and a message along the lines of "if you want to see more articles from [insert name], signup for her monthly newsletter here".

Blogging and guest blogging is a subject for a whole other book, but just for a bit of guidance, here are a few top tips:
- Do your homework and have a look around relevant blogs. Can you see posts from guest bloggers? If you're not sure, make contact with the blog owner and ask if they accept posts from guest authors.

- Tell them a little about yourself and send them some links to other articles you've written.
- Suggest article titles you have in mind and let them choose what appeals to them and their readers.
- If they publish your post, thank them!
- Keep in touch and build that relationship.

Other online tools

There are countless other online services that will collect email addresses on your behalf that you can use at a later date to promote your services. Here are just two examples:

- **Eventbrite** - or similar event software will capture the user's email address as part of the event registration process. You can then access these emails to inform them of future events or other promotions you may be running. So if you host events, workshops, seminars or open days, try using Eventbrite to streamline your registration admin and add to your email lists at the same time.

- **Webinar software** - such as GoToWebinar (www.gotomeeting.co.uk/webinar). You're probably thinking 'why would I us webinar software?' Well, if you have knowledge to showcase and you want to build your followers, webinars are a great way to get in front of lots of people across the globe at the same time. Webinars are short, 1 hour, seminars that people can access through their computer and listen live. There are free options out there too if you find GoToWebinar too pricey - try AnyMeeting (www.anymeeting. com).

This software should allow you to export a list of webinar attendees and add these to your mailing lists for future campaigns.

Offline methods for building your list

As well as utilising modern technology to grow your list of subscribers, you can still use some of the more traditional methods that can work just as well.

Here I'll outline just some of the methods I have used, or have seen being used, in the past to grow a list of subscribers successfully.

Point of sale

If you have a physical shop where you see customers face-to-face, you can use the sale process as an opportunity to capture more information about the person making the purchase.

I recently purchased a pair of boots from a local shoe shop. While the cashier was placing the boots into a bag, she slid a form across the counter and asked for my details that would be entered into a prize draw. The prize was to win my height in shoes, so I was obviously going to enter! The form was also clear in that by filling in my information I was likely to receive marketing emails from this company in the future, but I would be able to unsubscribe at any time.

This was a simple way to collect customer information. An attractive prize was offered which would appeal to the customers of a shoe shop, and the shop assistant was proactive at giving customers time to fill in their details. She could have given me something to take away and complete at home, but the return rate would be much lower as people forget, misplace things and become otherwise occupied with more important things in life!

Telephone

If you don't see customers face-to-face, but deal with them over the phone, this can also be a good opportunity to take down some more details while you are talking with them. Ask them for their email address and let them know that you'd like to keep in touch via email and ask if that is okay with them.

Don't say you're adding them to a bulk mailing list - this sounds so impersonal, and you'll probably find people aren't always happy about that. If you make it clear that you'll be sending them relevant information that will be of interest to them, they are more likely to agree to be added to your list.

Trade shows and exhibitions

Do you exhibit at local and industry trade shows? If you have ever visited a business conference you will be familiar with the business card goldfish bowl, which seems to appear on every stand you walk past (usually right next to a bowl of 'help yourself' sweets!).

These vessels are a way of gathering people's information (from their business card) with minimum effort. All the passerby has to do is throw in a card. In return, there's usually a prize draw for a hamper or bottle of wine.

Of course, you could use a data capture form, like I discussed for point of sale, and have this on your stand. If you wanted to get even more hi-tech, email software like MailChimp would give you a signup form that you can have running on your tablet computer for people to enter their details. These details are then automatically added to your mailing lists. Check out the Chimpadeedoo app in the Google Play or Apple Store.

I've also seen conferences where each attendee is given a name badge with a QR code printed on it. A QR code is a square barcode that can contain various pieces of information such as website addresses, telephone numbers, links to social media accounts or even just a plain text message. Exhibitors then have a barcode scanner on their stand and can scan attendees that visit the stand. The QR codes, in this case, contain the contact information for each attendee that can then be added to their databases.

Networking events

Networking events are a great place to exchange business cards with like-minded business owners. You may also connect with your contacts on LinkedIn too. If so, you can export your LinkedIn contacts in to a spreadsheet that can be easily uploaded to your email marketing software.

To download your connections from LinkedIn, go to **Connections** and **Keep In Touch**. In the top right corner, you should see a cog that says **'Settings'** when you hover over it. Click on this to reveal your advanced settings where there is a link on the right-hand side of the screen that says **Export LinkedIn Connections**. LinkedIn changes its interface regularly so if you're having trouble locating this link, try doing a search on Google or in the LinkedIn Help Centre.

Just be aware that they may not always be potential customers, so you need to think about the content of your emails when contacting them. Rather than sending them details of your services, trying to make a sale, you could opt for a more informal newsletter which just lets them know of recent projects, and PR you have had in local press or just general news and top tips.

It's also good practice to send an initial email to

let them know that you plan to email them in the future. You can do this when you connect with them on LinkedIn. They then have the option to decline the emails. This means you won't be emailing people who don't want to receive it.

Purchased Lists

If you're struggling to build a list of subscribers and you're in a hurry to start your email marketing campaigns, you may consider purchasing a list of email addresses that have been opted in to receiving email from third parties such as yourself.

These lists can be very targeted as you should be able to specify the types of businesses or consumers you want to reach. You can target by location, company size, contact within the company (such as Financial Director or HR Manager).

If you choose to purchase a list, make sure it's from a reputable source and that they are registered with the relevant authorities such as the DMA (Direct Marketing Association). You do not want a list of emails that have been harvested from websites - these are built using computer programs that scrape content from the internet and collate lists of emails it finds. These have not been opted in to receiving third party emails, and this could put you at risk of prosecution.

There's a lot of negativity surrounding purchased

lists, particularly around ethics and whether or not it should be more tightly regulated. There's also the argument that the people on these lists are unfamiliar to you, the purchaser, and as such they will be less likely to react in a positive way to receiving your email.

I have worked with clients with purchased lists of emails that have worked well in helping them achieve their goals. It's important to bear in mind that the recipients don't know who you are, so the content of your email needs to be tailored to this audience.

You also need to make it clear how they can remove themselves from the list if they wish to do so. The last thing you want is a few angry recipients who report you as a spammer. The more people who do this, the more chance there is that your email will get blocked and filtered into the junk folder for other recipients too.

Best Practice

When you have a signup form on your website, you are relying on the person submitting their email address to know what they are signing up for, be the owner of that email address, and be a genuine person. This isn't always the case so most email software providers will incorporate what's known as a 'double opt-in' to the signup process.

A double opt-in is where once an email address

has been submitted, the person signing up for the newsletter will receive an email thanking them and asking them to confirm the subscription by clicking a link within the email. Once this link has been clicked, they are, in effect, opting in twice and their email address is then confirmed as being genuine.

This is not a legal requirement but is considered best practice. If you're using email marketing software, they will take care of this process for you, so it's not something you need to worry about, but it's worth being aware of. If you're unsure whether your email software does this as part of the signup process, check their help or support area.

Data Protection

If you already have a database of names and email addresses or are planning to build one and you're based in the UK, you need to consider data protection and whether you should be registered with the Information Commissioner's Office (ICO).

The ICO is the "UK's independent authority set up to uphold information rights in the public interest, promoting openness by public bodies and data privacy for individuals" (https://ico.org. uk/). The Data Protection Act 1998 states that all organisations, sole traders and other businesses register with ICO unless they are exempt.

To check whether you need to register, you

can take a short self-assessment on the ICO website that will take you through some multiple choice questions (see: https://ico.org.uk/for-organisations/register/). Depending on how you answer these questions, you'll be given an answer as to whether you are required to register or are exempt.

The cost to register (at the time of writing) is just £35 for the year, so if you're unsure, it's best to register than risk not doing so.

If you're based outside the UK, you may need to register with a similar organisation in your country, so I would advise you to seek advice on this.

This chapter should have given you some ideas on how to grow your list of subscribers. I've also covered some points you need to consider with different methods of collecting data and also the legalities you have to adhere to in the UK. It's important to get your email marketing efforts off to the best start as you never get a second chance to make a first impression!

I've also mentioned, as I have in the previous chapters, about using email marketing software. You may think that this is something you don't need as you can just email people through Outlook, Gmail, Hotmail or whichever email service provider you use, but in the next chapter I'll tell you why you should be using dedicated software for this.

Chapter Four:
Why should I invest in Email Marketing Software?

In this Chapter I'll look at the pros and cons of using Outlook and other email service providers like Hotmail and Gmail to send your email marketing campaigns and compare them to the benefits of using dedicated email marketing software.

First of all, don't be put off by the term 'software'; you don't need to be technical at all to use most of these platforms. You don't need to download or install anything either as these platforms are all based online. You simply visit the website and login to your account like you would a social media platform. All your files, email templates, images and previous campaign reports are stored in your account for you to access wherever you are, as long as you have an internet connection. This makes them more flexible if you work from different computers.

Pros and Cons of using Outlook (or similar)

Most of us will use a program like Outlook to send and receive emails every day, so in some respects it appears to make perfect sense to continue to use Outlook to send our email marketing campaigns. This can get us into some difficulties further down the line, so let's look at why this might not be such a good idea:

Pros

- Outlook is already installed on your computer
- It's familiar to you, so you don't need to learn anything new
- You don't have to pay for each email you send
- It may look more personal if the email is sent from an individual's account

Cons

- **Outlook will often set a limit on the number of emails** you can send in one go; meaning you would have to send multiple emails to get the message to everyone on your list, and this would become a laborious task as your email list begins to grow.

- **If someone wanted to unsubscribe** from your list, you would have to have a system in place that would let them do this. This could be by replying to the email with 'unsubscribe' in the subject line. The downside to this is making sure you act on all of these requests and make sure you don't email them again.

This may be not be an issue if you only have a handful of people on your list, but when your list gets bigger, and the number of unsubscribers goes up, then you could get into difficulty.

I have worked with email databases of over 100,000 records and even with a low percentage of people unsubscribing, that could still amount to 2-300 unsubscribes each time an email is sent. With a manual process, it would have taken someone hours to remove these people in time for the next email campaign.

The danger here is that you don't keep up with the requests, and you end up emailing people who have been asked to be removed. This is where you could be breaching the law and could find yourself in trouble.

- **Reporting on your campaigns** is very difficult if you're using Outlook. You'll need to keep a manual record of how many emails you sent.

To track whether people opened your email you would have to either request a read receipt (please don't be tempted to do this, apart from annoying most recipients, you could just clog up your inbox), or get a little more technical and use a small image file and tracking code. This option is fiddly and means you need technical help to set up the campaign.

If you wanted to track people who clicked on links in your email, you would need to generate tracking code for each link, paste this code into your email template and have access to a Google Analytics account to monitor what was happening.

This will add a lot more time to setting up the campaign and will also mean you need help to set up the links and be proficient at interpreting Google Analytics reports too.

If you want to know whether someone has made a purchase or submitted an enquiry as a result of your email campaign, you will need to ask them where they heard about you and hope they remember and answer honestly!

- **It's easy to be blacklisted** and labelled as a spammer when sending through Outlook, or similar. This is because your email server, where the emails originate from, has no relationship or previous history with the ISPs (Internet Service Providers). The ISPs then see your bulk email as being potentially a spammer trying to send unsolicited emails to a large number of people. To prevent you from doing this, they can add you to blacklists that will make it difficult for your emails to reach anyone.

If you've read the above list and still insist on using Outlook, please, please, please, use the BCC field to address your recipients. Never paste your database into the 'To' field. This will send your entire list to your entire list and could be seen as a breach of privacy. Imagine receiving a bulk email from a company that has pasted your email into the 'To' field along with everyone else's email. Not only can you see all of their contacts, but all of their contacts will have your email address too.

While I was working for a company (and in charge

of their email marketing) a colleague decided he would send a bulk email to his database of around 400 businesses. He chose not to seek my help and instead used his Outlook account as he thought it would be more personal, and he could copy in his line manager so he could see the email had been sent.

Unfortunately, he simply pasted his entire list into the 'To' field and hit 'Send'. His line manager then approached me to say he thought something was wrong and asked if there was anything I could do to recall the message. I had to break the news that there wasn't much I could do given the time that had passed, accept to issue an apology.

The line manager then decided to email my colleague to let him know that he'd made a mistake by pasting the emails into the 'To' field and in future should use the 'BCC' field. Unfortunately, rather than starting a new email conversation, he simply hit 'Reply All' and sent his email.

Needless to say, the entire database was emailed a second time, this time with a slight telling off for the first email!

Outlook is a great tool, but where bulk emails are concerned, it's best to stay well clear and opt for dedicated software that would never let this happen!

Benefits of Email Marketing Software

Email marketing software is designed with the sole purpose of sending bulk emails to a database of subscribers. It, therefore, provides a better solution than using Outlook or Hotmail to send your emails. Let's look at some of the benefits:

- **You can send an unlimited number of emails** depending on your account and the plan you have chosen. Email marketing software will package its services based on the number of emails you send each month, the number of emails in your database or on a pay-as-you-go basis. Most providers will have a plan to you suit your needs and can cater for 'big senders' too. I've worked with clients sending 100k+ emails each month and the email software provided a reliable and very cost effective way of doing this.

  Your recipients will also receive an individual email addressed to them, rather than an email sent to 'Undisclosed Recipients' or something equally impersonal.

- **You can easily personalise your email**, so your bulk mailing looks a little less impersonal. This works by placing 'merge fields' into your email template. A merge field is simply a small piece of code that tells the software to add the information from your database. This could be a first name, so you can address the recipient by name. It could be the company they work at, or even details of the last order they placed with you, or the last time you spoke to them. Any information you have in your database can be transferred into your emails and you don't have to do this manually. Once the merge field is inserted into your email, the software does all the work for you. Kind of like doing a mail merge in Microsoft Word.

- **The ability to unsubscribe is built into each email** you send, without you having to change your email or remember to add an unsubscribe link. Because of strict anti-SPAM laws, email marketing software providers make sure that none of their customers can use the software for sending SPAM and that they adhere to the relevant regulations. This takes away some of the headaches of maintaining your database.

- **Unsubscribes are automatically removed from your list.** This means that it's impossible for you to email someone who has asked to be removed, giving you peace of mind that you're not accidently going to upset anyone by emailing them something they've explicitly asked not to receive.

- **Bounced emails are removed from your list too**. Bounced emails are when the message is returned as being 'undeliverable'. You may have seen this when emailing someone new, and you get a report back to say the email hasn't been delivered. This can happen if the email address is incorrect (typo, change of name, no longer using that email address etc.) or sometimes it can be because their inbox in full and cannot receive any more emails.

What you don't want to do is continue to send emails to these addresses, especially if you're on a pay-as-you-go package where you are charged for each email you send. Otherwise you're being charged for emails that are never going to be delivered. The great thing about email software is that it will remove these emails from your future campaigns, so you don't send to them again.

- **Reporting on your email campaigns is easy** with email software. Every time you send an email, the software will track how many people open the email, how many people click on links within the email and which links they click on, as well as the number of emails that bounce and the number of people who unsubscribe.

It will even let you see which individuals opened the email and who clicked on each link. This gives you a better understanding of how your email has been received and who it has appealed to. It can also alert you to potential issues within the email that you may wish to address next time you send out a campaign. For example, you may see that hundreds of people click on a link to contact you or submit an enquiry, but when you check your inbox, not one person has followed through and sent you a message. This could be because the link was broken or your enquiry form wasn't working correctly. Either way, you'd want to take a look at this and see what the issue was.

On a more positive note, your reports may show that there was one particular link within your email that was very popular. This could tell you that this is the kind of content people are looking forward to receiving, so you could use this to determine future content for your email campaigns.

- **Being blacklisted shouldn't be a problem** as email software providers build and establish relationships with Internet Service Providers (ISPs). ISPs know that software providers place restrictions and perform manual checks on customers using their software to send emails, to make sure that it's not being used for SPAM purposes. Therefore, emails sent from their servers almost come with a passport to say they are legitimate, so please let them into the inbox!

This doesn't guarantee that they will get into the inbox, as there are other factors, which I will cover in the next chapter, which can get your email filtered into the junk folder if you're not careful.

With all these benefits, there must be a downside, right? Well as the saying goes 'There's no such thing as a free lunch', and yes, you may have to invest some of your hard-earned pennies into email software, however, it's not as much as you think.

MailChimp (mailchimp.com) is probably one of the more popular services for solopreneurs and small businesses as it offers a free package for those that have a database of less than 2,000 email addresses. So if your database is still small, you can use their software completely free.

It's also one of the more user-friendly interfaces and is a lot less daunting than some of the software I have used in the past. It also comes with heaps of pre-built, attractive templates that you can use and customise; meaning you do not have to build something bespoke, which could incur additional costs from a graphic designer or web developer.

It's worth noting that the free packages often come with limited functionality. I, for example, wanted an email software package that I could use to send automated emails to new subscribers and even multiple emails over the course of several weeks. These are known as Auto-Responders and are not part of the free package on MailChimp, so to get this feature, I had to upgrade to a monthly payment plan.

If you don't qualify for the free package because your database is too large or you want additional functionality, you could opt for a pay-as-you-go package with any number of providers (try searching for 'email marketing software' on Google, there's hundreds to choose from). These are perfect if you don't plan to send emails out regularly (more than once a month) as they will just charge you for what you use in the form of email credits. These cost around 1p per email for smaller lists and the price drops the more emails you send.

If you do plan to send more regular emails, it often works out cheaper to go for a monthly payment plan. This will allow you to send emails more often for a set fee, so you can keep an eye on your expenditure. It also means that if you had some urgent news that you wanted to get out to your list, you could easily send an additional email without incurring additional costs.

Although the benefits of email marketing software far outweigh the costs, I know some of you are sat there reading this thinking, 'but I only have 50 or 100 people on my list, so it's easier just to send them through Outlook'. Wrong! How are you going to provide an unsubscribe link and manage these request as your database grows? How are you going to grow your list without sign up forms that automatically populate your database.' How will you know whether your email actually reached the person and if they acted on it?

For me, it's a no-brainer, you need to use email marketing software no matter what size your list is, to keep track of what you're doing and also to be able to upscale in the future. When I signed up for MailChimp, I had four emails on my list and 3 of them were mine! You have to start somewhere, and MailChimp is as good a place as any!

In the next chapter I'm going to get a bit more practical and show you how you can give your emails the best chance of landing in the inbox (and not the junk folder) and how to get people to actually open the email and not just hit the delete key!

Once you're tracking email open rates with your email software, you'll want to know why some people open their emails, and others don't, so read on to find out more.

Chapter Five:
How can I get my emails opened?

It's the one million dollar question - how can I get people to open my emails? Unfortunately, there's no guarantee that your email will make it into the inbox and get opened by the recipient, but there are steps you can take to give it the best chance.

It's important to bear in mind that there are a number of factors that can affect your open rates. For example, if your list is 'warm' (i.e. they are existing customers or prospects that have shown an interest in your services in the past), then you will find that your open rates are much higher than if you had bought a list of email addresses that belong to people who have never heard of you before.

Also, open rates vary across different industries and can also be affected by the content of the email. For example, if you're a charity, community group or social enterprise and you send out weekly newsletters with 'good news' stories, you'll probably see a higher open rate than someone running an e-commerce website who sends out emails each week to advertise products.

With this in mind, let's look at some ways in which you can get your email into the inbox and encourage your recipients to open it.

Avoiding the junk folder

Trigger words

The words you use in your subject line can have an effect on whether your email goes into the inbox or is identified as SPAM and gets filtered into the junk folder. Email service providers will read the subject line of the email and, if they think it represents a SPAM email, they will do their best to filter it.

Some of these trigger words are shown below. It's worth pointing out here that using SPAM trigger words does not guarantee that your email will be marked as SPAM, but it does mean it is more likely to be labelled as such. You should also be aware that these words trigger the SPAM filter when they appear on the subject of the email and not the email content itself, so don't think you have to avoid these words altogether.

Here are just a few of the words to avoid, for a definitive list see: http://bit.ly/triggerwords

SPAM trigger words

Money	Buy	Dear	Lose weight
Earn	Free	Friend	Stop snoring
Credit	Order Status	Hello	Guarantee
Loans	Quote	Lose	All natural
Income	Full refund	Miracle	Risk free

Money-back	No hidden costs	Click here	Urgent
Profits	Your income	Deal	Medicine
50% off	Get paid	Offer	Cures Baldness

Most of the words above will look familiar to you. You've probably received emails in the past that are what I would consider SPAM, and they usually focus on finance, weight loss and pharmaceuticals. There are a few less obvious trigger words like 'beverage', 'stainless steel' and 'Nigerian' - mainly because of the spate of SPAM which circulated in previous years regarding the transfer of money from a bank account. Many of these emails are phishing scams, linked to fraud and money laundering as well as SPAM.

A phishing scam is where an email prompts you to visit a website or reply to the email with your bank security details. These can be from someone who pretends to be your bank, PayPal or someone in another country who would like to send you a huge sum of money. Be very careful when opening these emails, and never click on the links in the email.

Take a look at the list above and see just how many words there are. Some are very generic words like 'get' and you may be thinking, 'how on earth can I write a subject line for my email without using one of these words'. Well, don't worry, avoiding these words is ideal, but there are other factors that SPAM filters take into account when an email is received.

Address Book

You may have a list of contacts in your address book. I'm not talking about that little pocket sized book with lettered dividers here, I'm talking about the address book or contacts lists that form part of your email software, such as Outlook, Yahoo, Gmail, Hotmail, etc.

These contacts should be people you know and trust and who you have a pre-existing relationship with. Because these people have found a way into your personal address book, it's assumed that you want to receive emails from them. Therefore, your email service provider will make an extra effort to land these emails in your inbox, so you get to see them.

This is how you would like the emails you send to be treated, so ideally, you would want your email address to be included in all of your recipients' address books. While it's not always possible for everyone to add you to their address book, you can certainly ask people to add you.

One way to do this is to add line of text to your emails that reads something like:

"To ensure you receive emails from us in the future, please add info@yourdomain.com to your address book."

I can't guarantee that your recipients will do this, but it doesn't hurt to ask them nicely!

Images

Images make emails stand out from the plain text emails you receive a lot of. It also gives you the chance to brand your emails to match your website, business card and other printed materials.

Having images in your email has its advantages, but it could also have disadvantages too.

An email that contains lots of images or even just one large image is traditionally associated with sales emails and this can sometimes affect the deliverability of your campaign.

While this is a secondary reason emails get picked up as SPAM, it's worth bearing in mind if your campaigns suffer from a low open rate.

Getting the email opened and read

Targeting

One of the biggest mistakes people make in marketing, in general, is getting their targeting wrong. The same applies to email marketing. It's vitally important that you know who you are targeting and how best to engage with them. It's all about getting the right message to the right person at the right time.

I will use another marketing model here known as the 3 Ms. The 3 Ms stand for Market, Message and Medium.

So to start with, you need to think about your **Market** - this is your target audience who you are trying to reach. Who are they? What characteristics do they have? You can use some of the characteristics listed below to build up a picture of your target audience:

- **Age** bracket (e.g. 16 - 24, 25 - 34 or 65+, etc)
- **Gender**
- **Location** - are they based in the UK, in a particular region, or globally
- **Marital status**
- **Family situation** - no children, young children, or grown up children who have flown the nest.
- **Job Title** - Human Resources Manager, Financial Director, Cleaner
- **Industry** (if you're targeting businesses) - manufacturing, healthcare, coaching
- **Company size** - number of employees or turnover
- **Device usage** - smartphone users or predominantly desktop users (you can get a lot of information like this from Google Analytics reports if you have it installed on your website. If you don't, it's free software, so it's worth investigating (www.google.com/analytics).
- **Previous purchases** - if you run an e-commerce site, or even if you don't, you should have a record of what people have purchased from you in the past. This can give you a better idea

of what they like and what they are likely to buy in the future.

For example, as a life coach, you may find that your typical client (it doesn't have to apply to each and every client you have on your list) looks something like this:

Female, aged 45 - 60, self-employed, with older children, iPad users

Or perhaps you're a freelance graphic designer and you work with small local businesses; your typical client may look something like this:

Owner/Managers, aged 35-60, catering and hospitality industry based within 50 miles of Bristol, predominantly desktop users.

Or you may be a sales coach or consultant working with larger companies, in which case your typical client may look something like this:

Sales Directors/Managers, financial services industry, turnover greater than £5 million, 50+ employees.

By building up a profile of people on your list, you can use this when deciding on your ***Message***.

Your message is basically the content of your email, the articles you include, how you address the recipient and introduce your content, and also your call-to-action (the action you want your recipients to take next, whether that's to pick up the phone and call you or click on a link and visit your website).

If the life coach I introduced above was to create an email campaign aimed specifically at her target audience, the campaign should perform well and, providing she constructed a catchy subject line (more on that in a second!), she should see a good open rate.

If, however, the same email campaign was sent out to the prospects and clients of the sales consultant, he would most likely see poor results and a low open rate. That's because the email simply wasn't targeted correctly.

Your message needs to speak to your audience and engage with them. You need to be able to identify what will make them open an email, whether that's a problem that they have and you can solve, a product you know they will love, or even some relevant news that will affect them.

It's also worth considering how people came to be on your mailing list. If they signed up for your newsletter on your website or they are current customers, they will already have a relationship with you and hopefully know what you do and how your services can help them or their business.

If, however, you purchased a list of email addresses, you won't necessarily be known to the recipients. They may not be familiar with your brand, your business or the products and services you offer. You, therefore, have to tailor your message to these recipients, making sure you introduce yourself and what you do before trying to sell, sell, sell.

Once you have an idea about your message, you can then think about how to present that message. This is called the **Medium**.

In traditional marketing, you would look at the medium as being something like TV advertising, radio, magazine advertising, social media, email, PR or some other medium by which you can market your products. As this book is solely focused on email marketing, I will use this step to look at how you format your email campaign.

For example, your email could be a:

- **Sales letter** - the purpose of this is to generate direct sales or enquiries from your campaign. This would be best suited to your business if you know that the majority of people on your list are past customers or have shown an interest in your services in the past. For this email, you would need compelling content to show your audience that your product or service will benefit them. You'll also need a strong call-to-action to get them to click through to your website and make a purchase, submit their details or pick up the phone and call you.

- **Newsletter** - probably one of the more common emails we get in our inboxes, this provides us with an excellent way of keeping in touch with our clients and prospects without selling to them all the time. A newsletter could be packed with useful articles that will benefit the recipient, but also show you to be an expert in your field.

One client I worked with sold insurance, but rather than just emailing their customers once a year at renewal, they sent out a monthly email that they call their 'e-magazine'. This contained lifestyle articles, product reviews and the odd article around how to avoid an insurance claim.

This can be transferred to other industries too. For coaches, why not email your clients with top tips for stress management or goal visualisation. For business consultants, keep in touch with your prospects by sending out regular articles about improving workflow and time management. For web designers, you can let your clients know about new design trends, making sure they know that you're on the ball so when they decide to invest in a new website, you're top of their list!

- **Survey** - asking the opinion of your email recipients is a great way to start to engage with them. Your survey could be about your customer service, or finding out what they want from your services in the future. You can even use a survey to ask them about how they want to be contacted - ask them how often they want to be emailed and what content they enjoy reading.

You can use free software to do this such as SurveyMonkey (www.surveymonkey.com) which will allow you up to 10 questions and 100 responses on the free package (at the time of writing).

If you want more flexibility, try Google Forms (http://www.google.co.uk/forms/about/). Google will let you create a form online and send a link to your email list. You can then download the results into a spreadsheet for analysis. Because Google Forms is part of Google Docs, you can also allow access to others to work on the same form and edit it from multiple computers, providing you have internet access.

- **Bulletin** - this is a quick way to keep your clients and other email contacts informed about what's happening either within your organisation or in your industry as a whole. A bulletin could be your Christmas opening hours, the announcement of a new website, or a change in your privacy policy or an important piece of legislation which affects your clients.

- **Lead nurturing** - I'll admit this is marketing jargon! Put simply, lead nurturing is when you have collected someone's email address, probably through the course of negotiating a sale, and you follow up with that contact via email to give them a nudge in the right direction.

As an example, imagine you're a social media consultant, and you have a free download on your website that gives *'10 Top Tips for Facebook Domination'*. As part of the download process, the recipient is required to give their email address in exchange for the document. Once they have downloaded the document and have had a chance to read the contents, now's a good time to send a lead nurturing email with a message along the lines of:

Thanks for downloading '10 Top Tips for Facebook Domination'. I hope you found the tips useful and have had chance to implement some of them already. I'd just like to reach out and let you know that if you have any questions or would like some help in developing your Facebook strategy further, I'm just on the other end of the phone.

Kind regards
Steve
+44 (0)1234 123456

- **Recommend a friend** - probably the best marketing you'll get is that which comes from the mouths of your happy clients! Word of mouth is a hugely powerful tool and your customers are often better at selling you than you are. So utilise this with an email campaign designed to get your happy customers recommending you to others.

Some people choose to incentivise their customers with a discount or credit off their next purchase or even a small gift like a bottle of wine or shopping vouchers. That said, you don't always need to incentivise people. If you have a good product or provide an excellent service, your customers won't hesitate to help you out and recommend you to their friends, family or business contacts.

It can be so much more satisfying (and less time-consuming) to build your business on referrals than have to go out and find new customers yourself.

The above examples are just some of the ways you can use your email marketing to get to the right people with the right message. By going through this process, you'll be making sure that your emails are targeted and relevant. Relevancy is key to getting your emails opened. If your email doesn't look like the content will be relevant to the recipient, they probably won't bother to open it, and you could have your email deleted.

From field and subject line

When your email lands in the inbox, your recipient is likely to see the 'From' field and the subject line first. They will often use these two pieces of information to determine whether they want to open the email, so let's look at each of these.

'From' field - this is where you say who the email has come from. It will usually be your name or your business name and should be something that's recognisable to the recipient. If they see that an email has come from someone or an organisation they know (and trust), they are more likely to open the email. It's also important to make sure you're not misleading people with the 'from field', i.e. pretending to be someone you're not.

Subject - this short line of text is often what makes or breaks an email marketing campaign, and there are several factors that you need to bear in mind:

- *Length* - it's recommended that you limit your subject line to around 50 characters including spaces. This is because they are often cut short when viewed in the inbox. This limit works well when people read emails on their desktop computer, but when they view them on their mobile, the subject line is often cut even shorter to fit on the tiny screen. Therefore, I would recommend trying to keep your subject lines around 30 - 40 characters and make sure that the important bit is at the beginning, in case it gets cut off!
- *Trigger words* - as I covered in the previous section. Even if you manage to avoid the

SPAM filter and get your email into the inbox, there's still a chance that saying something that seems 'spammy' (or, indeed, 'phishy'), could ruin your chances of getting your email opened.

- **Content** - the content of your subject line is your opportunity to entice your recipients to open the email. You need to give them a reason to click. What will they gain, learn or achieve by reading what you have to say. How will this email make their lives easier, better or more fun?

- **Fulfil the promise** - whatever your subject line, you need to make sure that what it promises, the email content can deliver. You may think that creating a really clever subject line that gets people to open your email, but has no relevance to the content of the email, is a good idea; and yes, it may inflate your open rates, but what you really want from your campaign is to create engagement or generate sales. You also risk annoying a lot of people if they click to open the email expecting one thing and it's something completely unrelated.

I would always recommend trialling different subject lines to see which gets the better open rate. You can do this in your email marketing software by splitting your list in two and sending one batch an email with subject line A and the other batch an email with subject line B. This is often called 'A/B' or 'Split' testing and can give some really useful insights into how your audience interacts with your emails.

Best time to send

Just like a phone call, there can be a bad time to receive an email. The timing of your emails plays a big part too in determining whether your email will get opened or ignored. Think about your typical day in the office. There will be times when you can sit down and dedicate some time to going through and reading your emails, and there will be times when you simply don't have the time, and they have to take a lower priority. This is often when you're more inclined to hit the 'delete' key if the email doesn't look like it's important or relevant for now.

A lot of what I'm going to show you next is common sense, but sometimes it's good to see it spelled out in black and white for reference!

Business to consumer (B2C) emails

Assuming your customers have a regular full-time job, working 9am to 5pm, the best time to send your emails is when they are not at work:

> Tuesday, Wednesday or Thursday from 5pm to 8pm
> AND Friday evening to Sunday afternoon

This works well for most B2C emails. However, it may be different for your target audience. If, for example, they are stay-at-home mums or students who spent more time at home during the day, it may be better to send emails earlier in the day. You may also be targeting people who work shifts like nursing staff, so their day is never a typical 9 to 5 shift.

You have to use the information you have about your audience to decide on the best time to send.

Business to Business (B2B) emails

Again, I'm assuming your contacts work 9am to 5pm and have weekends off, so the best time to send B2B emails is:

> Tuesday, Wednesday or Thursday at 9.30am
>
> AND Tuesday, Wednesday or Thursday at 1.30pm

You want to avoid sending B2B emails on a Monday as this is when people arrive back in the office after the weekend. They have lots to organise for the week ahead and probably a full inbox too. They are, therefore, more likely to prioritise certain emails and your newsletter or sales emails may not make the cut.

You should also avoid sending on a Friday too. This is because Friday is typically the day when you want to get all your important jobs finished before the weekend and anything new that lands in your inbox is likely to be ignored until the following week unless it's really urgent. Then your email falls victim to the Monday morning inbox clear out.

Sending your emails on a weekend isn't a good idea as there is probably no one there to receive the email. It will just sit there until Monday where it will suffer the same fate as the Friday email!

The two specific times given here are based on general patterns of people checking emails. The theory is that people check their emails first thing when they land in the office. By 9.30am, they have cleared out all the rubbish and are just left with the important emails to deal with or, with any luck, an empty inbox. If your email lands at this time, it will get more attention from the recipient and is less likely to get lost in all the email clutter.

The same theory applies to sending emails at 1.30pm as this is around the time people return from lunch and check their inbox once again.

As I mentioned for B2C emails - it can really depend on the type of businesses you are targeting. If, for example, you are sending an email campaign out to trades people who often work six days a week, sending on a Friday might not be such a bad thing. Or, you may be targeting people in the hairdressing profession whose weekend is Sunday and Monday rather than Saturday and Sunday.

To summarise the answer to 'when is the best time to send emails':

B2C - when they are at home
B2B - when they are at their desk, and their
inbox is empty

In this chapter, I've gone through how to create campaigns that will help you to bypass the SPAM filter and land your email in the inboxes of your recipients. I've also covered the key areas you need to think about in order to get your recipients to open your email and read what you have to say.

You should now be confident in creating a campaign that will get you the results you want. But how do you know if it's been a success and what can you do to make improvements for next time? I'll be covering this in the next chapter!

Chapter Six:
How do I interpret my reports and make improvements?

Reading reports and using the information you find in them to make adjustments and improvements to your campaigns is vital if email marketing is going to be successful for your business.

No matter which email marketing software you choose, you should have the ability to see reports that will show you how many emails were sent, what percentage were opened and the number of clicks on the links within your email. You'll also be able to report on emails that are returned undelivered (bounces) and people who ask to be removed from your database (unsubscribes). Some email software providers also allow you to connect your social media accounts so recipients can share the content through their Facebook and Twitter accounts. If this is the case, your reports will show how many people shared your email through social media too.

In this chapter, I'll look at some of the terminology used in the reports and how to determine whether your campaign has been a success. I'll also look at the issues you can face that can affect the success of your campaigns and actions that you can take to rectify them.

Open rate

The open rate for your campaign will be shown as a percentage and is simply calculated by dividing the number of people who opened your email by the number of emails that were sent. So if you sent out 5000 emails and 1000 people opened your email, the open rate of your campaign would be 1000 divided by 5000 which equals 20%.

Email software is not always 100% accurate when calculating open rates, so it is worth bearing this in mind when you view your reports. The software detects an email has been opened when a small image, placed in your email, is downloaded from their server. This image is often transparent and not visible to the recipient and won't affect the design of your email. Because it relies on images being downloaded, if your recipients use Outlook, for example, and don't download the pictures, this may mean that it is not recorded as an opened email.

In short, what this means for your email reports is that the number of people opening the email may appear to be lower than the actual number, so the stats may look a little on the pessimistic side.

Generally speaking, you'll want to see the highest possible open rate for your email campaigns. While getting a 100% open rate isn't impossible, it's only likely if you have a small database of people who know you well and want to receive your emails.

Clicks or click through rate

Once someone has opened your email, there may be several actions you wish them to take. You might want them to click through to your website to make a purchase or read an article on your blog. Either way, you should have links within your email for people to click. These links can be simple text links or images, such as buttons.

Email software will track when each link is clicked. It will also track who clicked each link, and you should be able to download a list of people who responded to each call-to-action.

Depending on your campaign goals, clicks are a good sign that your email content has been compelling enough to generate interest.

Bonus tip! If you can download a list of the people who clicked on certain links within your email, say to a particular service you offer on your website, you can send a follow-up email to these people, knowing that they are already interested and offer them additional information and more reasons to buy or make an enquiry.

Bounces

When you send your email campaign to a large number of people, there may be some emails that cannot be delivered. If you were sending these from your Outlook account (or similar), you would get a report back to say the message wasn't delivered along with a reason. This is often because the email address was incorrectly typed, but can also happen if the email account no longer exists or the inbox of the recipient is full and cannot receive emails until others have been deleted.

These undelivered emails are known as 'bounced' emails as they bounce back to the sender. In an ideal world, we wouldn't see any bounces in our campaign reports, but in reality they are inevitable, especially as our databases grow, and lists get older.

There are two types of bounced emails - 'hard' bounce and 'soft' bounce. Hard bounces are where there is a permanent issue with the email recipient, such as the email address doesn't exist or if the email server refuses incoming mail. Soft bounces are the result of temporary issues with the recipient's email, such as the inbox being full.

SPAM/Abuse reports

Some email marketing software will keep a record of how many people mark your email as SPAM. Lots of abuse reports can lead to you being unable to send emails in the future, so it's important to avoid these by only sending emails to people who are likely to be interested in your services.

Unsubscribes

As I've covered in previous chapters, it's important to allow recipients to remove themselves from future email campaigns. You can do this automatically when using email marketing software as it will add an 'unsubscribe' link to each email that is sent.

In your reports, you will be able to see how many people click on the link to unsubscribe. As with bounces, you don't want to see any unsubscribes in our reports, but they will happen from time to time.

What constitutes a successful campaign?

Before you can look at fixing issues with your campaigns, you need to decide whether anything needs fixing!

Depending on your industry and the quality of your database, your open rates and click through rates will vary. If your database is made up of people who you know and have either worked with before, or who have shown an interest in your services, you should find that your open and click-through rates are a lot higher than someone who has bought a list of email addresses of people who are unfamiliar with you and your organisation.

MailChimp publishes the average response rates, broken down by industry in their Email

Marketing Benchmarks report: http://bit.ly/ mailchimpbenchmarks.

Here are a few examples taken from that report:

Industry	Open Rate	Click	Hard bounce	Soft bounce	Abuse reports	Unsubs
Consulting	20.40%	2.64%	1.20%	0.91%	0.03%	0.30%
Creative	23.90%	3.13%	1.38%	1.10%	0.04%	0.38%
Beauty	19.91%	2.34%	0.58%	0.57%	0.05%	0.34%
Restaurant	25.01%	1.68%	0.39%	0.34%	0.03%	0.30%
Prof. Services	22.05%	2.88%	1.18%	0.94%	0.03%	0.33%

The figures shown were correct at the time of writing and show data for just a few industries. For an up to date summary of key benchmarks for all industries, visit -http://bit. ly/mailchimpbenchmarks. All data is taken from MailChimp account holders.

Looking at the data here you can see that an open rate of 20 - 25% is considered average with anything over 25% being considered very good. If your open rates fall below 20%, you may want to look into why this may have happened.

Click through rates vary, but average between 2% and 3%. These can be affected by the number of clickable links you have in an email.

Bounce rates average between 0.5% and 1%.

This can be dramatically increased if you are emailing old data as many email addresses will have changed or no longer exist, and you may experience a higher than average bounce rate. Luckily, email software will remove these email addresses from your next campaign so your bounce rate should drop from your second mailer.

Abuse and SPAM reports are very low, and you're unlucky if you receive them. Although there will be people who perceive your email to be SPAM, the most common reaction of people is to just delete the email.

Unsubscribe rates should also be lower than half a percent. People unsubscribe for different reasons. Some will want to be removed because they find the emails irrelevant. Others will just want to reduce the number of emails they get in their inbox each week, so will unsubscribe from the non-urgent newsletter type emails. Others may unsubscribe if you email too often.

My husband was having difficulty locating an email in his inbox so I pointed out that it may have been filtered into one of the different tabs that Gmail introduced called 'Promotions'. He'd never checked this before, so he opened the tab to find it full of promotional emails. Scanning through the list it was clear to see that a certain electrical company was emailing him every other day! That's three or four times a week! Although technically this wasn't SPAM as he had agreed to receive these emails when making a purchase, this would certainly be considered annoying for the majority of recipients and will no doubt lead to many unsubscribing.

Your aim is always to create and send emails that are targeted and relevant to the recipient. By being consistent with doing this, you will avoid the unsubscribes and abuse reports.

How do I address a low open rate?

Before I delve into how you can improve your open rate, let's look at the reasons why people don't open emails.

It's useful here to think about the many emails that land in your inbox each day, but you never open them. They usually get deleted for some reason or another whether it's because you feel it's not relevant or you are just too busy to open and read what appears to be a non-urgent sales email.

So how do you avoid this happening to the email you send?

First of all, you need to consider how your email appears when it lands in the inbox. Usually, the recipient will see who the email is from and the subject line. That's two areas where you have the opportunity to influence the recipient into opening the email.

The name in the 'from' field tells the receiver who the email is from, but it also tells them whether that person or organisation is familiar to them. If you see an email in your inbox from a friend or family member, you are more likely to treat that email as important and open it. If the email you receive appears to be from a company you have never heard of, you are less inclined to treat the email as important and less likely to open it.

Therefore, when you send emails to your list, we want people to recognise who the email is from. It's also important that we don't mislead people into thinking the email is from another source. For example, if you're an accountant, you shouldn't try to make your email appear more important by changing the 'from' field to HMRC or a similar government body.

You should keep the 'from' field consistent with each mailing you send. Whether you use your company name or your name, it should be the same each time you send an email. This will build a relationship with the recipient so they recognise your name and know that the email is from someone they already know.

Your subject line is the next opportunity to get people to open your email. This is where you want to create intrigue and curiosity so that people will be driven to open the email and find out more.

So to recap from the previous chapter, here are

my top 5 tips for creating great subject lines:

1. **Keep it short** - subject lines are often cut short when they appear in the inbox on desktop computers, but even more so when viewed on a mobile device. I'd recommend crafting your subject lines to be less than 40 characters including spaces.

2. **Important stuff first** - Because your subject line may get cut off, it's a good idea to say the important stuff first! For example, if your subject reads something like this:

   "Spring/Summer Newsletter No.234 - How to build a successful business."

   Consider switching the content around to look something like this:

   "How to build a successful business - Spring/Summer Newsletter No.234"

   This will ensure that the recipients will see what the email is about if the end of the subject line gets cut off.

3. **Ask a question** - this can be used in different ways, but asking a question is a great way to inspire a sense of curiosity in your readers. Here are a few examples:

   "Did you know that most businesses get their marketing wrong?"

"Have you seen the new eBook that could change your life?"
"Are you aware of what the new EU law means for your organisation?"

4. **Personalise it** - as I covered in previous chapters, it's simple to personalise your emails, and it's also possible to personalise the subject line.

   I ran an email campaign for a client where the main aim was to get as many people to open the email as possible and take part in a customer service questionnaire. Traditionally, emails were sent out as a newsletter with the subject line being a similar format that would have been familiar to recipients. I wanted this particular campaign to stand out as being more important, so personalised the subject line, kept it short and asked a question:

   "Heather, can you help?"

   Of course, I used a merge field for the first name so each recipient would receive an email addressed to them.

   This campaign achieved open rates of over 40%, compared to their previous average of around 25% and the response to the survey more than met expectations.

5. **Don't mislead** - Although the subject line is a great opportunity to grab people's attention

and make them open email, it's not a good idea to promise something that you cannot deliver in the email content. Yes, you may see an increase in your open rates, but that's unlikely to be reflected in click through rates and you could see an increase in abuse reports or unsubscribes.

Crafting the perfect subject line can be a case of trial and improvement (nothing's ever an error if it leads to better things!). I can highly recommend trialing different subject lines by splitting your email list in half and sending one half one subject line and the other half a slightly different subject line and then reporting on which email received the best open rate.

MailChimp offers A/B testing as a feature of its service, as do most other email software providers, so make use of it!

A low open rate can also indicate that your email never made it into the inbox and may have been filtered into the junk folder. If you think your open rates are too low, make sure that you haven't overdone it with SPAM trigger words in the subject line (see Chapter 5).

How do I address a low click through rate?

The number of clicks you get on each campaign can be affected by a few things. First of all, make sure that you have included clickable links within your email - sounds really obvious, but I've seen campaigns that look like a complete disaster, but in reality, there was no opportunity for people to click on anything!

Secondly, the quality of your content and its relevancy is key to getting people to click through to your website. I recommend including a catchy headline with a teaser paragraph that gives the reader a reason to click through to your website for more information. So don't give everything away in the content of the email.

Creating content that is relevant and useful all comes down to how well you know your audience and what issues they face, what interests them and what they will find useful.

How do I address a high bounce rate?

Bounces can happen for a number of reasons, and many, if not all, of these reasons, are out of your control when you are sending email campaigns.

What you can do, however, is focus your efforts on replacing those emails that no longer exist with new emails.

To do this, you can download a list of email addresses that have bounced from your email campaigns and, if you have alternative contact details for them, you can contact them and explain that their email address appears to be invalid and ask for their current details so you can update your records.

If you don't have alternative contact details, now's the time to re-read Chapter 3 and look for ways to build your list to replace the bounced emails.

How do I address a high unsubscribe rate?

Unsubscribes can seem like quite a personal thing, especially if you are emailing your contacts, but it's important to take a step back and realise that people unsubscribe from emails for various reasons, and it's probably nothing personal!

To minimise the number of unsubscribes, think about the content you are sending and the subject line you use. Is it relevant to your recipients? Does it sound interesting?

As with bounced emails, unsubscribes can be out of your control, but it's a good time to replace those emails with new subscribers, so turn your attention to building your list.

If you find a very high percentage of people are unsubscribing it could be because your list is cold (i.e. they don't know you), or it could be because you are sending too many emails. Take this opportunity to send a survey and ask what kind of content your database wants to receive and also how often they want to receive emails.

This chapter has been all about reading and

acting on the data you find in your campaign reports. If you want email marketing to work well for your business, it's important that you remain consistent in your approach and regularly review how well campaigns perform.

When you spot figures that look like they could have done better, you should be reviewing why that has happened and how you can learn from it the next time you send an email.

Summary

Email Marketing still plays a huge role in generating new business and repeat business for many organisations, so it's just too much of an opportunity to ignore.

It can come in many forms and doesn't always have to be a sales email that can so easily be marked as SPAM. Think about using email to survey your customers, send them industry news and useful information as well as encouraging them to recommend you to their friends and contacts. Email can also be a great way of nurturing leads and following up with people who have shown an interest in what you do.

Emails can also be a superb way to cross sell other products and services you provide, increasing your revenue and maintaining that client relationship. You will also have people on your database who don't necessarily follow you on social media or visit your website often, so email provides another way of distributing the content you produce for your blog.

Using email marketing alongside blogging and social media, you could start turning those followers and fans into paying customers.

All you need is a database of email addresses to get started. These could be your LinkedIn contacts, your customers, a list you've built from trade shows or even a list you have purchased.

Providing you make sure your recipients have opted-in to receiving emails, you are fine to begin sending regular updates.

Due to its cost effective nature, email marketing provides the perfect way for solopreneurs to promote themselves and build relationships with their clients and prospects for very little investment. With software such as MailChimp, business owners can set up and manage regular email campaigns free of charge while their database remains below 2000 emails. As your list grows, you can upgrade your account, but never pay more than around 1p per email.

Email communications may have lost favour in recent years due to the rise of social media, but the reality is that email can and does provide a better way of selling to your contacts. Social media is something every business will benefit from embracing, but it should in no way replace email marketing and other forms of marketing that have proven to be effective.

Whilst email marketing has been noted as being more effective at acquiring new customers, it's also a great way to keep in contact with existing and past customers and letting them know what you can offer and just generally keeping in touch. By making contact with your clients on a regular basis, you're bound to be at the forefront of their minds next time they or someone they know requires your products or services. Repeat business is much easier to come by than new business!

If you haven't used email to promote your services in the past, I encourage you to take the plunge! If you have been using email for a while, I hope this book has provided you with enough information to take your campaigns to the next level. It should also enable you to assess how well they are working for you and give you hints and tips to grow your list and make them perform even better.

I welcome all feedback, questions and comments, so if you'd like to share or ask anything, then please feel free to get in touch with me via email (heather@skitti.sh) or through any of the social media channels listed in the 'About the Author' section.

OODLEBOOKS
Online Book Store